Upon hearing *Ready to Die* by The Notorious B.I.G., Felipe Joe felt fear. A vivid, wild picture of life in the streets, the album ignited what would become a lifelong love for hip-hop. Raised in Chicago with his older sister and parents, Felipe Joe spent his early years obsessed with sports. After dropping out of high school at 17, he later received his GED and would go on to earn a Bachelor of Arts in Creative Writing from Columbia College Chicago. *My Journey Through Hip-Hop* is his publishing debut.

Felipe Maldonado

My Journey Through Hip-Hop

AUSTIN MACAULEY PUBLISHERS®
LONDON * CAMBRIDGE * NEW YORK * SHARJAH

Ordering Information
Quantity sales: Special discounts are available on quantity purchases by corporations, associations, and others. For details, contact the publisher at the address below.

Publisher's Cataloging-in-Publication data
Maldonado, Felipe
My Journey Through Hip-Hop

ISBN 9798886938876 (Paperback)
ISBN 9798886938883 (ePub e-book)

Library of Congress Control Number: 2024907186

www.austinmacauley.com/us

First Published 2024
Austin Macauley Publishers LLC
40 Wall Street, 33rd Floor, Suite 3302
New York, NY 10005
USA

mail-usa@austinmacauley.com
+1 (646) 5125767

I would like to give thanks to my mother Laurie, father Felipe, and sister Angie. As well as the rest of my family and friends for their support throughout these years. Also, acknowledgement goes to everyone at Austin Macauley Publishers who helped during this process.

Bronx, New York, 1970s

Some people say South Side
Others feel it began in the west
Roots grew at 1520 Sedgwick Ave building complex

Created by African Americans
And Latinos along with Caribbeans
An immigrant from Jamaica gave deejay turntables their
first spin

Clive Campbell better known as Kool Herc
With help from his Sister Cindy gave a culture birth
House parties started this artwork

Playing off crowd reactions
Old records mixed in popular dance songs—how it
happened

Four pillars got this established
DJ's plus turn tabling
MCing became rhymes
Graffiti writing a sign
B-boy dance style's formerly time.

Evolution of Hip-Hop

Both Afrika Bambaataa and Grandmaster Flash
Were influenced by the very near past
We also can't forget Grandmaster Caz

They used innovative methods
To utilize two songs during their beat breaks as a new weapon

Sounds from what seem like galaxies away
Consider renegades like Malcom X along with MLK
Nothing from that age would ever be the same

All deserving of handclaps
For visual dreams with passion

Which wouldn't blow away like any white line
Only got higher baby during those times

Like up your nose or through the veins
Music changed our brain

The Last Poets spoke words, then came beats
Saying hello to all kids from the street.

Mainstream

As hip-hop spread through the five boroughs of NYC
Shouting during their DJ's set arose MCing

From Coke La Rock and Clark Kent
Grand Wizzard developed scratching a record under the
needle
Becoming a serious threat
Rock Steady Crew break-dancers expressing themselves
By Jo Jo plus Jimmy D using those legs

Sugar Hill Gang gave this genre their first big commercial
break
What a *Rapper's Delight*
Then Kurtis Walker became the first artist a major label
signed
New Jersey was one of the main factors
With Mr. Magic's *Rap Attack* on WHBI

We can't forget about her—Wendy Clark—better known as
Lady B
Considered one of the first females rapping on this scene.

Featured

This era was dedicated to the peace
Party people moving their feet

It started showing growth
First appearance on TV was by Kurtis Blow

Gave us a break down
Throw your hands high
Wave them from side to side

Then everybody screams
Clap those palms with rapture
Rappers plus pop art became a team.

Worldwide

Gigolo Rapp represented first tracks
By Disco Daddy put on for Cali
Taught everyone it's time to party

Get their freak on the floor
Stomp real hard

From west to east and north, all the way towards the south
This culture proved having a *Wild Style*

Film backed by Fred Brathwaite
Explored those days of Lady Pink, also Daze

Which led to more like an international tour
With Afrika Bambaataa, Fab 5 Freddy, and Double Dutch
Girls.

Madness

Street life and violence
No longer would those stories stay silent

One of the OGs was Ice-T
But what he talked about was nothing sweet
Growing up around friends hustling

They helped him realize *Rhyme Pays*
A key reason developing gangster rap inspired by LA

Those killers will *Body Rock*
Cold Wind even when that temperature is hot

Los Angeles lifestyle made into movie roles
Like *Colors* depicting an artistic view of South Central.

Beginning of the Golden Age

New stylistic came into existence

Mic prodigies with fresh technology
For instance, use of the drum machine
Augmented samples brought us groups like Run D.M.C.

Started by three men considered a radical band
Opened doors to political rap

Rev was ordained as *Reverend*
Jam Master Jay lays peacefully in heaven

Along with Darryl McDaniels
Was our first group to have a certified gold album

Part of this generation mid school
Created producers like Larry Smith and Rick Rubin
Lyrics, also instrumentals, were faster moving.

Importance of a Group

There was a Public Enemy
Which included Flavor Flav and Chuck D
Also Professor Griff with DJ Lord
Either went platinum or gold for their first four
Long Island is where they formed

Words of criticism of the American media
Active interest within urban communities
Made politically charged music seriously concern
Lessons for all to be learned

Another pairing was KRS-One along Scott La Rock
Boogie Down together before being shot

Teacha continued doing music
Hits like *Sound of da Police* a stop the violence movement
Still *Criminal Minded* in the Bronx you could find them

Can't forget Rakim and Eric B.
Consider the best DJ—MC team

They got *Paid in Full*
Only 16 years old, he got into this game when most were worrying about following rules

Influential also skilled nephew of Ruth Brown
Singer plus an actress of R&B
Greatest lyricist went solo after breaking up in early 1993.

Positive Rap

Connected ties to the Universal Zulu Nation
Native Tongues spoke their very own language
Lyrics written with good nature

Very much Afrocentric
Pioneering sounds of jazz and electric
A few groups were at its center

A Tribe Called Quest ft. Ali Shaheed, Q-Tip, and Phife
Dawg
Another member was Jarobi White though in 1991 was no
longer together
There was also those Jungle Brothers

All of them became buddies
Linked from natural love of art while having fun not for
money
They shared spirituality plus ideas about modern living

Some consider these guys conscious or alternative
Trends began turning again.

Music Manifest

During this time of duos, then came a Guru
Beside DJ Premier they had *Mass Appeal*
Made hardcore sounds
Gang Starr was born *No More Mr. Nice Guy* around

One of Wild Pitch Records best
Label that also featured Lord Finesse

Leading the D.I.T.C. Crew
Diggin' in the Crates with former partner Mike Smooth
Future was bright including Showbiz, Diamond D, O.C,
went Buckwild
Can't forget Fat Joe and Big L too

All about this business like EPMD
Making dollars most acclaimed doesn't come free

Erick Sermon and Mic Doc Parrish
Broke up twice in the 90s not long after a major signing.

Center Stage

Listen to those fans screaming
Artists began selling out arenas
This movement became real
Once rappers started getting endorsement deals

Albums changed people's perceptions
Driven by singles, that's what caught everyone's attention

Looking back who could see the impact
An agency based on musical rap called Def Jam

A lot of noise created by LL Cool J also Beastie Boys
This company opened doors for Cold Chillin Records and
Tommy Boy
Soon both would rise to prominence
Because of Rick Rubin plus Russell Simmons were
dominant

Tones also manner restructured quick
Marketed along with upcoming stars like Slick Rick soon
Mike D, MCA, plus Ad-Rock wanted to jump ship

Their departure wouldn't hurt
It help finding 3rd Bass Pete Nice and MC Serch.

International

From British-born Rick, *The Ruler*
All this way to Barbados with Doug E. Fresh beat-boxing
smoothest

Both were part of *The Show*
Gifted wordplay and lay backflows

Storytelling wordsmith enter
Tales of great adventures
Lead to a smash-selling record.

Phenomenon

Superstars were bicoastal
Now with attitude because of the west coast

Originated with these few fellas
MC Ren also DJ Yella
When Ice Cube spoke it was a good day
Bravado brought by Eazy-E
Final touch from Dr. Dre

Once they got going, there wasn't any stopping
World's most dangerous group *Straight Outta Compton*

This industry had something to fear
A storm been brewing for years
Epicenter considered New York; it started here

Movement began changing course
Places like Bay Area came up Too Short
Put his city on map
Being *Born To Mack.*

Elevated

Microphone fiend greatest lyrically
Fans follow this leader wherever he leads

Truly was unique his rhymes took this game to new levels
Resemblance that of a poet Rakim's words were essential
Boasting with awareness about any cultural issue

Big Daddy Kane suave and fierce
Closest rival through verses had emerged

Brooklynite delivering friendly or scathing thoughts into that mic
Ready for battle against all fights

Long live two legends who could spit!

Having Fun

1989 Grammy's first rap performance of the year's best
Went to Fresh Prince and Jazzy Jeff

Two friends from Philly, both acting silly
Something, *Parents Just Don't Understand*

One had those hooks other with charisma also a charm full
look
Both appeared to have this certain lighter flare
Eventually, they would end up in Bel Air

MC Hammer *Let's Get It Started*
Road led to mega stardom

For a while, he was loved by an American public
Seemed like no one, not me or *U Can't Touch This*
But all good things come to end.

Women Write

Crazy it may seem
Females had respect for years like Shante or Lady B
They were good back then since *The Real Roxanne*
Hold their own with any man had to salute them

Not just looking pretty, she rocks all cities
Show nothing but love because The Sequence would *Funk
You Up*

Equality not anything lesser
Made room on that table for Salt-N-Pepa
Notice all fellas magical step forward like Spinderella

Prime time, they helped *Push It*
Women's visibility refine our world's looking

MC Lyte could really flow
Brought mainstream change in hip-hop gender roles

Against any opponent she could stand
Attack Lyte as a Rock very brash

Young leader would inspire others like Queen Latifah.

Foundation

Building blocks were being laid
Mc Shy D was representing that A

Atlanta Georgia
Comin' Correct became very important
On Luther Campbell's Skyywalker, he did his recording

Down in Houston you would find those Geto Boys
The Sire Jukebox, Raheem, and Prince Johnny C
Along with others previously employed

Group did reshuffled
After *Making Trouble*
Second version most influential
Southern act renewals

Buzz didn't stop
On Rap—A lot

Got bigger it seem because of Scarface plus Willie D.

Debut

An important launch was a TV show reflecting back
Called *Yo! MTV Raps*

Created by Ted Demme and Peter Dougherty
They helped sharing hip hop stories

First aired Aug 6, 1988
Showcasing videos to an audience who caught on late
Way of life could finally be seen by the whole United States

Rural areas could look in
Seeing through a wider lens

Before only the biggest stars got noticed
Local radio programs were completely ignoring.

Relevance

Some performers from the last decade kept grinding
Maintaining connection with fans by making songs that are
timeless

Salt-N-Pepa continued to represent
Considered first ladies of the 90s
Kept dance floors filled but also educated those about safe
sex

Other musicians as well carried on
Beastie Boys wouldn't be *Sabotage*
Their message spoke loudly
Stayed true riff heavy and rowdy

They weren't the only one who were outspoken
Public Enemy thought 911 was really joking
Wasn't fair to them ambulances response toward black
areas

Former member of N.W.A.
Ice Cube was first breaking away
His own career started controlling
Released brilliant tracks about shagging and smoking

A Tribe Called Quest had a *Low End Theory*
For leaders of the new school like Busta Rhymes, this was stirring.

Series of Changes

There was already bona fide stars
Pop stations portray non-threatening rap during this start

When they played them at all
Restricted airplay but not having big hits wasn't that cause

Sampling became an issue
Biz Markie had to face the law

Though it didn't make their genre weak
Huge songs put it firmly on top of music's heap

Position which it never took for granted
Spreading beyond urban heartlands

Into bedrooms of suburban youth.

Contribution

Movements continued to grow
Like that trio called De La Soul
In high school originally forming
Lyrics considered quirky

Kept Native Tongues on track
Significant too early stages like artists Mos Def

They weren't the only independent leaders
New style by a group that was *Naughty by Nature*

Helped from Jackson 5's *ABC*
Are you down with *O.P.P*
Group arose through poverty.

G-Funk

It was time to *Regulate* like Warren G
With Nate Dogg, a good night in Long Beach

Ultimate party tune
Add little *Gin and Juice*
Began the rise of iconic artists like Snoop
Just needed weed, women, and booze

Nuthin' but a 'G' Thang
Production by Dr. Dre

His rise couldn't stop it
Slipped into this limelight debuting *The Chronic*

Revolutionary style
More accessible format for airwave sounds.

Rebellious

This would change the course in history
N.W.A. claimed a top spot on Billboard
Watershed moment death to hard rock
Ascent for hip-hop became one of its greatest victories

Momentum wouldn't stop
Most vital artist called Tupac
Addressed civil matters that plagued city blocks

Symbol against resistance
Voice for activism
Inspired by experiences in American prisons

Law enforcement couldn't hold him down
It was set *2Pacalypse Now.*

Counterpart

New York was always part of the theme
Before they owned this business now beginning to cling
Commercially struggling keeping up and competing

But far from stagnant, they had plans
Arrival of a gritty group Wu-Tang Clan

Perfect timing their city was in danger
Outstanding crew gave us 36 Chambers
Dollar, dollar, bills they help change it

Filthy and guttural grooves
Ol'Dirty Bastard raucous plus rude
Also sampled collection of Kung Fu

Central act these killer bees would sting fast

Became known so *Protect Ya Neck*
Reinvented the structure earned respect.

Local Talent

Legends already achieved success
LL Cool J was one the best

All he needed was a *Radio*

Still can rock those bells
Mama still says she'll knock you out

Some people are advanced
Biggie Smalls just needed *One More Chance*
Sean Combs gave him that
Along with Craig Mack
B.I.G. had a lazy eye and was fat
But there was none who had his swag

Stories told of grim content
Criminality, celebration, with hardship

Few were skilled at this
When Nas debut *Illmatic*

Paid dues waiting for a chance in that studio
When Rakim and Kool G Rap weren't working
Nasty would go in their booth recording material
Never released until being heard on Main Source's *Live at
the Barbecue*

MC Serch helped getting Kid Wave signed
A nickname way before *Half Time*.

Latino American

Proud Hispanic really loves rapping
It wasn't until Big Pun that Latins went platinum

Capital Punishment became Grammy nominated
Unique breath control heavy use of alliteration
Notable technical efficiency
Having exceptional rhyming scheme multi-syllabic

Emerging from the underground
Was on a record label considered Loud

But spent half decade with Terror Squad
Fat Joe found Christopher Lee Rios in Bronx

Let's go to South Gate
Were Cypress Hill was raised
Groundbreaking on Hollywood Walk of Fame

This band always advocated
For cannabis medical and recreational legalization

Some thought it was *Insane in the Membrane*
Ruff House they claimed.

Relocate

Shakur became so much more involved in war
Similar to what happened on stage at the *Source Awards*
This all begun when Death Row was sort

Suge Knight took a gamble like dice
Bailed Pac out of jail contract got scribed

Law breaking notoriety hadn't done his career no harm
Filming movies like *Juice* and *Poetic Justice* becoming a box office star

With Calvin Broadus turned into *2 Of Amerikaz Most Wanted*
Even accompanied by *Bad Girl* Madonna.

Gained Exposure

This industry was close to war
When Escobar let us know *The World is Yours*

A legendary tune describing his upbringing
Twist of *Scarface* movie as he seen it

Pete Rock and CL Smooth
Taught us truth with when *They Reminisce Over You.*

East v/s West

These two coast became involved within heavy rivalries
First double CD had *All Eyez on Me*
Death Row against Bad Boy feud would end tragically

Big Poppa was known as a showstopper

Life After Death would release just few days following his final rest
Eventually achieved certification going Diamond
2pac also would go on to have huge success
They share similar fate in ways which dying

One of them was shot at Las Vegas in a drive by shooting
Another gunned down going back to California both lives were ruin
But whose legacies continued because of their music

Brooklyn's own Jay-Z was Notorious protégé
Others got involved over this beef like Snoop Dogg and Mobb Deep.

The Southern Way

Appearing from *Underground* were these Kingz
Alias was Pimp C and Bun B

Started as amateurs like those nights inside Apollo
Their style *Too Hard to Swallow*

In the beginning had *Pocket Full of Stones*
Later on *Big Pimpin'* with Hov

Wasn't no stopping them
Sippin on Some Syrup alongside Three 6 Mafia

That will Hypnotize Minds
Approach was Mystic always would grind
DJ Paul even took piano lessons at one time

A few members could rep this gang
Most popular had to be Juicy J

Isn't a gimmick
When Master P founded No Limit

Only select people follow their dreams
Generated personal basketball league
Music he would *Get Away Clean*

Not everyone becomes a rapper
Also makes into the NBA with *Hornets plus Raptors.*

Misfits

Two good men
From another world like *ATLiens*
In Lenox Square they met

Both would follow the same path
Organized Noize as OutKast
Among Goodie Mob formed Dungeon Fam

They worked hard putting together a *Player's Ball*
Andre' 3000 and Big Boi would take off

Achieved critical acclaim
And commercialized success also came

Experimenting with funk as well psychedelic
Incorporating techno, it really was special.

Entrepreneur

Singer, songwriter, and executive
Own career began after the death of a friend

An eye for talent was Puff's early challenge

At Uptown before he developed *No Way Out*
Relationship with J. Lo only higher Diddy's profile

Most recognizable figures
Bottled Ciroc liquor

Assisted flourishing Mary J. Blige as well as Jodeci
Had people wearing Sean John clothing.

New Dynasty

Born on December 4th
Eventually a billion would be Shawn Carter's net worth

Raised in Marcy Projects
Songs would become Jigga's vacuum after pops left

Growing up having an extensive record collection
Michael Jackson and Stevie Wonder played inside their house
All those sounds of Motown
Hustling on streets true calling was found

Drummed against kitchen tables
Years before Roc-A-Fella label

Creating was an obsession
Jaz-O influenced progressing

Reached a wider audience within this game
Featured in album by Big Daddy Kane
Teaming up together with Kareem and Damon

From out of the car selling music
To *Reasonable Doubt* giving leverage during distribution.

Hardcore

Prodigy alongside Havoc would make many classics
The Infamous joined forces with Lil Kim

Making a *Quiet Storm* and *Hell on Earth*
Murda Muzik those two were progenitors
Narrative of street life straightforward

They had this dark image
Probably from being *Survival of the Fittest*
Who stopped to listen was Q-Tip

Weren't *Shook Ones*
Neither was DMX beat-boxing for Ready Ron

After doing time in the criminal system
Earl Simmons began writing lyrics
Performed at rec centers for young children

Unstoppable force was *Born Loser*

The Lox helped with *Money, Power, Respect*
Initiated a strong buzz
Flesh of My Flesh, Blood of My Blood.

Mile to Success

Career didn't always seem *Infinite*
That changed placing 2nd in Rap Olympics

Teenager flowing inside clubs
Sold poorly at first continued working menial jobs

But caught attention from Jimmy Iovine
Turbulent childhood relationship with mother

Alter ego was Slim Shady

Chronicled hits about difficulty with Kim
97 Bonnie & Clyde
When Andre Young signed Eminem associates criticized
For hiring a white guy

Instant credibility *My Name Is*
Most controversial best-selling artist
Of early 21st century nobody doubted again

Brought beside Dirty Dozen
Fell into depression when Proof died

Marshall really loved him
Denigrated boy bands
Made history with Elton John what a *Stan*
GLAAD didn't like the gay icon's stance.

52

Battle Uniting Two Titans

There's history to how this story goes
Leading up into war of gladiatorial
Kicked off with jabs at first were subliminal
Recording meeting someone didn't show

Ultimately, this would *Bring It On*
At first, Jay-Z sampled a line from Nas

Dead Presidents It Was Written
Referencing luxury cars but they got *The Message*

Let him know *Where I'm From*
The City Is Mine, said young

Memphis Bleek dropped *What You Think of That*
Nastradamus would fire back

Got My Mind Right
Stillmatic would bring others towards this fight

Freestyle at Summer Jam
Diss grew the beef then

Hova released *Takeover*
Nasir replied with *Ether*
Who won this match people would say either

Things got *Super Ugly*
God Son must respond

But reconciliations *Black Republicans* teamed up surprised
our whole nation.

Sistas

Missy Elliott was *Supa Dupa Fly*
Before *Get Ur Freak On*
Apart of Swing Mob

Collaborating with Timbaland
For more than *One Minute Man*

Miss… E So Addictive
While *Da Real World* was *Under Construction*

After losing Aaliyah
4 My People she continued to *Work It*

Earliest woman inducted inside *Songwriters' Hall of Fame*

From Philly Let There Be Eve
First peeress of Ruff Ryders
Let Me Blow Ya Mind
Blossom Fetish clothing line
Co-host *The Talk* on CBS daytime.

Gangsta Lovin'
As Terri Jones in *Barbershop*, she was Back in Business.

Midwest

Across St. Louis Missouri
Materialized Lunatics like Murphy Lee

But their biggest star was Nelly
Who had a *Dilemma* with Kelly

Taught us *Country Grammar*
Would go *The Longest Yard* aside Adam Sandler

In some *Air Force Ones*
Had *Pimp Juice* if you wanted some

Getting *Hot in Herre* so *Move That Body*
Apple Bottoms for all those hotties.

Clash

Out of Queens
Set up a rival between

50 Cent and Ja Rule
Publicized dispute
Associate related to Curtis robbed Jeffrey
Orchestrating this plan he was accused

Prior to *In Da Club*
During an old video shoot Ja thought 50 was hating
Because their neighborhood showed him much love

Incident happened at The Hit Factory
Altercation left Jackson wounded from a stabbing

Done by someone connected with Murder Inc
Take that straight to the *Piggy Bank*.

Extraordinary

Dipset representing Harlem
Jim Jones straight ballin'

Cam'ron and Juelz
Few others as well

Had *Diplomatic Immunity*
Come Home with Me

Heading through Yonkers
Jadakiss was a problem
D-Block with Swizz Beatz the Monster

We Gonna Make It
DJ Clue aided in Fabolous getting famous

Take a moment to *Breathe*
Put together Street Family

Redman and Method
Blackout for sessions.

Generation Talent

Barack Obama said about Lil Wayne there's not many
Regarded highly by contemporaries

Commenced at age 12
Birdman saw skills
Joined Cash Money and really helped

Part of those Hot Boyz with Juvenile, Turk, and, B.G
Coined the phrase *Bling, Bling*
Rapidly would make *A Milli*

Told us *Tha Block Is Hot*
Human being I am not
Made her wanna lick a *Lollipop*

Constructed several mix tapes
Most entries surpassed Elvis Presley, the great

On list of hottest songs
Top spot Weezy does belong.

Chi-Town

Common gave this city *Resurrection*
Gained attention with Soulquarians

Love of My Life at a time was Erykah Badu
Glory original song as awarded won two

Including *Golden Globe*
Chicago place called home
Kanye West told us *Watch the Throne*
Before *Kids See Ghost*

College Dropout led to *Late Registration*
Succeeded reaching *Graduation*
Lupe Fiasco chief of 1st and 15th entertainment
Long way from recording in Dad's basement

Cool designing Reebok shoes
Had anti-establishment views

Put together *Food & Liquor*
Twista there was none who rapped quicker

Appearing on Do or Die's *Po Pimp*
Slow Jamz didn't go away swift

What an *Adrenaline Rush*
Get It Wet just to be touched.

Dirty South

Ludacris was Disturbing Tha Peace
But still kept *Southern Hospitality*
Asking, *What's Your Fantasy*

Back For the First Time
Had theater kind of mind

Jeezy gave Thug Motivation
Still needed a *Vacation*

Go Getta Who Put On
DJ Drama's *Trap or Die*

Spoke to our president warning about this Recession
T.I. lead a Road to Redemption
First though an *Urban Legend*

Did terms in county jail once for probation violations

Told women *Whatever You Like*
With Rihanna, *Live Your Life*

Never Scared, Let's Get Away; we can go anywhere.

Eureka

The Game surfaced playing in Compton
So did Kendrick Lamar gained recognition people found
themselves watching

An *Untold Story* about a *Good Kid, M.A.A.D. City*
LAX always stays busy

Learning from *The Documentary*
Was this Black Hippy

Each were apart of *Doctor's Advocate*
He just seemed to have that affect
Was *Born to Rap*

Damn acquired a *Pulitzer Prize*
Spoken word *To Pimp a Butterfly*
Lost an angel when Nipsey Hussle died

Slauson Boy from Crenshaw

Past before taking his *Victory Lap*
Heading *Higher*, that's just a fact

Bullets Ain't Got No Name
But another person does who aims
We all felt pain

Though life isn't a jog
It's really The Marathon.

Heartland

Kid named Cudi
Moved out of Ohio
Because a cool old man said he was funny
However this stranger really saw something

Worked hard *Day 'N Nite*
Until GOOD Music saw Mr. Rager strive

Passion, Pain, & Demon Slayin'
Welcome to Heartbreak

Everyone's *Paranoid*
Until they find that *Dark Sky Paradise*
Like Big Sean in Detroit

Ye said give me 16 bars short verse
Two years later joined his label, now that's *Bezerk*.

Self Made

Maybach Empire *Mastermind*
Notified us *The Devil Is a Lie*

And *God Forgives, I Don't*
I'm a Boss, Rick Ross
Like John Gotti *Teflon Don*
As DJ Khaled would say Another One

Port of Miami-Born-N-Raised
Brought cooperatively along Meek Mill with Wale

Back to Back much *Deeper Than Rap*
War Ready, Here I Am
Dreams and Nightmares at times *Going Bad.*

Showing Growth

Ready to Jumpman and imprint Freebandz
What a moment to be alive
Just *High Off Life*

Straight *Beast Mode*
Whenever they *Move That Dope*

Future reached *Astronauts' Status*
With *Tony Montana* also making *Magic*

Prevalent using auto-tune
Artistic tool reinvented Blues

Formally Tity Boi at the start
Later on 2 Chainz always though from College Park

One half of Playaz Circle boy got duffle bags
Feds Watching Supply & Demand

I'm Different in dabbing sweaters

Dropped *B.O.A.T.S 2: Me Time*
Everyone can relate… *No Lie.*

Royal Crown

Heritage Trinidadian birthed in Saint James
District town of Spain
Business woman and model put together *Super Bass*

Known for colorful wigs similar with costumes
Same as accents having a distinct flow

Nicki Minaj can't have her without an *Anaconda*

Cardi B kicked off astonishing career as an internet celebrity
But always had love for hip-hop
Aggressive lyrics in *WAP*

Thug chick attained multiple number-one jams *I Like It*

Both these females made history matching Lauryn Hill

During this fashion week party
Shoe was thrown at Nicki by Cardi

She felt for a while disrespect

Back to a tweet mentioning mothering skills about Offset and their kid

Differences linking them seems more than *Bodak Yellow* or *The PinkPrint*.

Next

Canadian manufactured mayhem
Prominent actor in a teen drama

Drake still had *Room for Improvement*
Come Back Season and *So Far Gone* seemed like illusions
Until *Thank Me Later* bonded a Young Money union

Nothing Was the Same
If You're Reading This, It's Too Late
Views have changed

Dancing doing the *Toosie Slide*
Crazy *Dreams Money Can Buy*
Will always be here *Forever* that leads all *Headlines*

On The *Come Up* was J. Cole
Speaking for Dreamville

Riding through Forest Hill Drive
Only *4 Your Eyez*
Going back to *Friday Night Lights*

A Star Is Born
Informed us *Love Yourz*

Blaza joined an *American Gangster*

Roc Nation
Nobody's Perfect but these two are on their way to greatness.